Lincoln Takes a Trip

I Talk You Talk Press

ISBN: 978-4-909733-69-6

www.italkyoutalk.com

info@italkyoutalk.com

CONTENTS

I Talk You Talk Press

CHAPTER ONE

Lincoln is looking at his computer screen. It is almost midnight. He is on Facebook.

I have a friend!

He is very excited.

Lincoln lives in a small town called Stamford. It is in Texas. He is 38 years old. He lives with his mother and owns a grocery store.

When Lincoln was a teenager, he went to high school in a nearby town called El Placido. After high school, many students went to university, or went to big cities to find a job.

Lincoln stayed in Stamford. He worked in his father's grocery store. His father died a few years ago. Lincoln owns the grocery store now. It is not very big, and Lincoln doesn't make a lot of money.

He spends his evenings on his computer. He loves Facebook. He hopes he can find old friends, and make new friends there.

Every evening, Lincoln takes out his yearbook from high school. It has the name and photograph of everyone in his class. He searches for them and sends friend requests. Usually, he doesn't get an answer.

Tonight, Lincoln searches for Eric Williams. There are a lot of Eric Williams on Facebook. Lincoln looks at the photographs. *Which one looks like the Eric Williams who was in my class?*

One of the photographs on Facebook looks a little like the photograph in the yearbook. Lincoln sends a friend request.

A man called Eric Williams is in his smart apartment in New York. He is looking at his Facebook page when he sees Lincoln's friend request.

What an idiot, he thinks.

Then he reads Lincoln's message.

He comes from Stamford, near El Placido! That is very interesting! I wonder if I can use him?

He answers Lincoln. ---*Hi Lincoln! Thank you for your friend request.*---

Lincoln is very pleased when he gets a reply from Eric Williams. He sends a long message explaining what he has been doing with his life since high school.

Eric does some research on the Internet. He finds the El Placido High School page. There is a lot of information about the school, and about the people who went to the school when Lincoln was a student there. He can look at the yearbook for 1999 online.

It will be easy to pretend that I went to that school. It will be easy to pretend that I am the Eric Williams that Lincoln went to school with. That person was interested in art and computers, he thinks.

So he sends a message to Lincoln. He says he studied art and computer science at university. Then he got a job in New York. He says he works for a travel magazine.

Eric and Lincoln exchange messages two or three times a week. Lincoln enjoys it very much. At first, he thinks Eric will be bored, but Eric is always interested.

Lincoln tells Eric all about his life. Lincoln takes photographs of everything, and sends them to Eric.

---*This is my cat.*---

---*Here is the new display in the window of my grocery store.*---

---*Here I am with my pickup truck. Every Thursday, I drive over the border into Mexico to a market to buy fruit and vegetables to sell in my store.*---

Eric is delighted. *This idiot is perfect! I can certainly use him,* he thinks.

CHAPTER TWO

Eric sends Lincoln a message. ---*Why don't you come and visit? We can have a great time together.*---

Lincoln is very pleased. He makes plans. He tells his mother he is taking a vacation. He asks her to look after the store for a week. He goes to Walmart and buys a bag for the trip. His mother asks, "Why did you buy a black bag? It looks like everyone else's bag. You will never find it at the airport. You need to put something on it, so you will know which bag is yours!"

Lincoln's mother knows a lot about travelling. She belongs to a travel group. Twice a year, she goes travelling with the group. They go to Miami or San Francisco. Once, they went to Hawaii. Lincoln drives to Mexico once a week, but he has never been anywhere else.

His mother ties a big pink plastic flower to the handle of Lincoln's bag.

"Now you will know which bag is yours," she says.

"But Mom, I have a name label on my bag! I don't need a flower!"

Lincoln thinks it is silly to have a plastic flower on his bag. He sends an email to Eric with a photograph of the bag. 'Don't you think this is crazy?' he asks.

Eric emails back. ---*I think it is a great idea. Your mother is a clever woman.*---

A few days before Lincoln leaves for New York, he gets an email from Eric.

---*I am in trouble. My magazine is writing a big article about travel in Mexico. We want to show pictures of souvenirs from Mexico. But I made a mistake. I forgot to order them. My boss will be very angry with me. Can you help me? When you go to buy fruit and vegetables tomorrow, can you pick them up for me? I will ask a friend to put the parcel in your pickup truck while you are at the market. Then you can bring it to New York when you come.---*

---*No problem Eric. I am happy to help you.*--- writes Lincoln.

Lincoln goes to the market in Mexico as usual. He buys melons, mangos, tomatoes, lettuces, hot peppers and corn. When he puts the fruit and vegetables into the back of his little truck, he sees a parcel.

That's not many souvenirs, he thinks. *It is small. That is good. It will fit in my bag.*

He drives back to the border between Mexico and the USA.

Everyone at the border knows Lincoln. He has been driving this route for many years.

"Hi Lincoln. How are you?" says the border guard, as Lincoln hands over his travel papers.

"I'm great, thank you, Abe."

Abe looks in the back of the truck. "Just the usual?" he asks.

"Yes. And some souvenirs. I'm going to New York for a week!"

"Good for you," smiles Abe. "Have a great time!"

He waves Lincoln through.

As soon as Lincoln gets back to the store, he unloads his truck. He takes the parcel home and puts it in his black bag. *I don't want to forget to take it. I promised Eric,* he thinks.

He sends an email to Eric. ---*I have your parcel. It's in my suitcase!*---

In New York, Eric calls his girlfriend, Marcia. "It's good! The idiot picked up the drugs in Mexico and took them through the border without any trouble. He will fly on American Airlines, from Dallas to LaGuardia on Sunday. His suitcase will have a big plastic flower on the handle. I'll send you a photograph of him, and a photograph of the bag. This is what I want you to do…"

Marcia listens carefully, and laughs. "You are very clever Eric! This will be easy!"

CHAPTER THREE

Lincoln is waiting to check in his bag at Dallas Airport. The line is long, and he talks to an elderly woman standing behind him.

"Where are you travelling today?" asks the woman.

"I am going to New York." Lincoln is proud to say this.

"I'm going to New York too. I'm meeting a friend there. She is coming from Rome."

Finally, Lincoln reaches the counter. He looks at the bags on the conveyor belt. No one else has a plastic flower on their bag.

Everyone will think I'm crazy. A man of my age with a plastic flower on the handle of his bag! he thinks.

Very quickly, he bends down and takes the flower off his bag. He drops it on the ground. When he has finished checking in his bag, Lincoln hurries to get a coffee before it is time to go to the departure lounge.

The elderly woman steps up to the counter. She steps on the plastic flower and picks it up. She gives it to the woman working on the counter. "This flower was on that man's bag. It must have fallen off."

"Which man?"

"The man whose bag you just checked."

"Oh. Which bag was it?" The counter attendant and the elderly woman stare at the conveyor belt. There are many black bags, and they look the same.

The attendant points to one of the bags. "That one. I am sure it was that one."

She ties the flower to the handle of the bag and smiles at the elderly woman. "Thank you. It was lucky that you saw it."

In the coffee shop, a very pretty woman comes to Lincoln's table and says, "May I join you? The coffee shop is so crowded today."

Lincoln looks around. There are many empty tables. *Why does she want to sit with me?* He thinks it is strange, but he is happy. He has never had a girlfriend, but he dreams of meeting the perfect woman. *Maybe she is my perfect woman. I am going to New York, and anything can happen in New York!* he thinks.

"Where are you going?" the pretty woman asks.

"New York," answers Lincoln.

I'm going to New York too!" she smiles. "Are you on the American Airlines flight?"

"Yes," says Lincoln.

"So we are on the same plane. Maybe we will sit next to each other."

She takes out her boarding pass. "I am in row thirteen, seat C."

Lincoln looks at his boarding pass. He is disappointed. "Oh, I am in row fifty-three. That's a long way away."

The pretty woman stands up. "Never mind. I am sure we will see each other when we get off the plane at LaGuardia Airport." She walks away.

Lincoln watches her. *She never drank her coffee!* he thinks.

Lincoln enjoys the trip from Dallas to New York. He has never been on a plane before, and everything is new and exciting. The elderly woman from the check in line is sitting next to him. Lincoln wishes it were the pretty young woman, but he talks and talks. She tells him her name is Clarissa. He tells her all about his friend Eric and his plans for his week in New York.

Clarissa is very bored. *I hope he will be OK in New York. He is like a baby, and New York can be a dangerous city,* she thinks.

Lincoln is waiting for the bags from his flight to arrive in the collection area at LaGuardia Airport, when he sees the very pretty woman again. The woman walks across to him. She must really like me! thinks Lincoln.

"Did you enjoy your flight?" she asks.

"Yes, very much. Do you live in New York? I am staying with a friend for a week. Maybe we could meet for coffee or a meal."

The young woman doesn't seem to hear him. She is staring at the baggage carousel. As soon as the bags start to come, she says, "Oh, I am so thirsty! I would love some water."

"I'll get you some!" Lincoln is pleased to help.

He walks quickly to the vending machines and buys a bottle of water.

As soon as he has gone, the young woman picks up the black bag with the plastic flower on it. She pulls off the flower and puts it in her pocket. Then she carries the bag out of the baggage claim area.

On the other side of the carousel, Clarissa is watching. *Why did she do that? Who is she? That is not her bag. That bag belongs to Lincoln, the very boring man from Stamford.*

Then she sees her own bag and forgets all about it.

Lincoln comes back with the water. He is hot and red because the vending machines were far away, and he hurried. But when he arrives back at the carousel, the young woman is not there!

He feels very disappointed, but he sees a black bag come around. *That is my bag,* he thinks. He checks the label. It says *Lincoln Berger, Stamford, Texas.* He carries it out into the public area of the airport.

CHAPTER FOUR

Eric told Lincoln ---*I will come to the airport to meet you. Wait by the Information Desk. I will find you.*---

Lincoln goes to the Information Desk and looks around. He can't see Eric anywhere. The airport is busy. Lincoln has never been in a place with so many people before.

He waits and waits. *The traffic in New York is very bad. Maybe Eric is in a traffic jam. Maybe he is stuck at work,* he thinks.

He is very tired. He didn't sleep well last night because he was so excited. His feet hurt. He has a headache because the noise and people are too much for him.

After an hour, he thinks, *Maybe I am in the wrong place. I'll call Eric and ask him where to go.*

He takes out his Smartphone and then…*I don't know his phone number! I'll send him an email from my phone.*

He sends an email and waits for an answer.

Clarissa is sitting in the airport. Her friend's flight from Rome is delayed. She has to wait. She has a book to read, but it is not interesting. So she is looking at all the people in the airport. There are families, businessmen, students and many international travellers.

She sees Lincoln. He has been standing by the Information Desk for a long time. *He said his friend was coming to meet him,* she thinks.

Then she remembers seeing the young woman take the bag with the flower on it.

That's strange. He has a bag. Clarissa is old, but she is very smart. *There is something wrong here. I think I will go and talk to him.*

She walks over to Lincoln and says, "Come and sit with me."

Lincoln looks worried. "I have to stay here. My friend is coming."

"It will be OK," says Clarissa. "You have been standing here for a long time. You must be tired. We can see the Information Desk, so we will see your friend when he arrives."

Lincoln is pleased to sit down. "Why don't you call your friend?" asks Clarissa.

"I don't have his phone number."

"Well, maybe you should take a taxi to his apartment."

"I don't know where he lives."

I am sure something is very wrong here, thinks Clarissa.

"Your name is Lincoln, isn't it?"

"Yes, that's right."

"Tell me, Lincoln. The bag you are carrying. Is it your bag?"

"Yes. It is. Look." Lincoln shows her the label - *Lincoln Berger, Stamford, Texas*

"OK. But where is the flower? When we were in the line at Dallas Airport, I saw you had a big plastic flower tied to the handle of your bag."

Lincoln's face is red. "I took it off and threw it on the ground."

"When did you do that?" asks Clarissa.

"When we were in the line to check in our bags," says Lincoln.

"Oh dear!" Clarissa laughs. "Do you know what I did? I picked the plastic flower up. I thought it had fallen off your bag. I told the person on the counter to put it back. I guess we chose the wrong bag!"

"I don't understand," says Lincoln.

"I don't understand either," says Clarissa slowly. "But I have an idea. Did you have anything special in your bag? Something valuable?"

"No! No! Just my clothes and some souvenirs."

"Souvenirs from Texas?"

"No. They are souvenirs from Mexico. I am bringing them to New York for my friend."

Oh Lincoln! thinks Clarissa. *This is very bad!*

She looks around the airport. She sees a man in a security guard uniform. She calls out to him. "Hey! You! Please come here."

The man comes to the seats where they are sitting. "Can I help you, Ma'am?"

"Yes. Please take this man to the airport security office. I want to report a crime."

"What!" Lincoln is very surprised.

"Sorry Lincoln, but I think your friend is a very bad person. You must go with this man and tell your story. I will come with you to help you."

CHAPTER FIVE

A taxi stops outside a smart apartment building in the middle of New York City. Marcia climbs out, and the taxi driver gives her the black bag from the trunk.

She takes the elevator to Eric's apartment. Eric is waiting for her.

"What took you so long?" Why are you late?" asks Eric.

"The traffic was terrible! We sat in traffic jams for about an hour."

"Did you get it?" he asks. "Did you get the bag?"

Marcia laughs. "Of course! It was so easy!"

"Great! And that idiot Lincoln is waiting for me at the airport with no bag! He might try to email me. But that's OK. I sent all those emails from the public library. I have taken down my Facebook page so he will never be able to find me."

Marcia takes the plastic flower out of her pocket and throws it in the air.

"Thank you, flower!" she laughs. "We will sell the drugs in the parcel for a lot of money and go and live in the Bahamas."

Eric opens the black bag. It is filled with men's clothes. He pulls the clothes out. There is no parcel.

"What!" he shouts. "This is the wrong bag!"

"No!" shouts Marcia. "It was the only bag with a plastic flower. It must be his!"

Eric picks up a shirt. "You saw his photograph. Lincoln is a big man. This shirt is too small for him. It's the wrong bag!"

He picks up his phone. "I guess he is still waiting for me at the airport. We must find him and get the drugs out of his bag! I'll send him an email and tell him to wait for me."

---*I am so sorry. I got held up at work, and my car wouldn't start. I'll be there soon.*---

CHAPTER SIX

Lincoln and Clarissa are sitting in an office at the airport. The head of airport security is sitting behind a desk. His name is Oscar Watts. A woman is standing by a big table. She is wearing a security guard uniform.

Lincoln is very nervous. He doesn't know why Clarissa wants him to talk to airport security. He wants to go back to the Information Desk and wait for Eric.

"It's OK," says Clarissa. She looks at Oscar's badge. "This man's name is Oscar. Tell him your story from the beginning."

"The beginning?" Lincoln doesn't understand.

"How did you meet your friend?"

"I was looking for people who were in my class in high school."

Lincoln talks about the yearbook and Facebook. He talks about Eric and Eric's job.

"We are good friends," he says. "Eric asked me to come to New York. I am here for a vacation. I don't know why he didn't meet me. Maybe the traffic is bad, but I am sure it is OK."

Oscar looks at Clarissa. "Why do you think something is wrong? Why did you say I must talk to this man? Are you wasting my time?"

Clarissa is angry. "No! I am not wasting your time. I am an old woman, but I am not crazy. Listen to me! I stood behind this man in the line at Dallas Airport. He had a big plastic flower tied to the handle of his bag. You know, many bags look the same. Some travellers put something on their bag so they can find it easily in the baggage collection area."

"My mother knows a lot about travelling. She told me to do it," says Lincoln.

Clarissa goes on. "After he checked in his bag, I saw the flower lying on the ground. I thought it had fallen off his bag. So, I picked it up and told the woman on the counter to tie it back on. We thought we found Lincoln's bag, but I guess we made a mistake. Later, when we arrived at this airport, I was in the baggage collection area. I saw Lincoln talking to a young woman. Then he went away. The young woman picked up the bag, took the flower off and walked away with the bag."

"I met her in Dallas," says Lincoln. "I think she likes me. She asked me to get her some water. But when I came back, she had gone. Maybe I was too slow."

"I am not going to say any more," Clarissa says to Oscar. "Maybe I am wrong, but I think you should look in his bag."

Oscar frowns. "I think you are wasting our time. But we are here, so…."

He says to Lincoln, "Sir, please put your bag on the table."

Lincoln picks it up and puts it on the table.

"Sir," says the woman from airport security. "Did you pack your own bag?"

"Yes!" says Lincoln.

She opens the bag and looks inside. There are clothes and shoes. She pulls out the parcel. "Did you put this parcel in your bag?"

"Of course!"

"What is in it?"

"I don't know. They are souvenirs. I don't know what they are. My friend Eric needs them for a photo shoot."

"Did he give you the parcel?"

"No. I picked it up in Mexico for him."

"I will open this parcel," says the woman. She takes a knife and cuts the paper and string.

Lincoln is very surprised. There is only one item in the parcel. "That's a piñata! It will be full of candy for children."

The woman cuts open the piñata and everyone can see the bags of white powder.

"There is no candy in this piñata," she says. "Only drugs."

Oscar looks at Clarissa. "I'm sorry," he says. "You were right."

Lincoln is very unhappy. He doesn't understand what is

happening.

"You said your friend's name is Eric. When did you last see him?" asks Oscar.

"Twenty years ago, in high school."

"Do you have a photograph of him?"

"No…." says Lincoln slowly. "There is only the photo in the high school yearbook. I sent him many photographs, but he never sent any to me."

"Where does he live?"

"In New York City. He never gave me an address."

"But you have his phone number?"

"No." Lincoln is feeling bad.

Then he feels his phone vibrate in his pocket. He takes it out. Suddenly he is very happy.

"It's Eric! He's coming now! He will explain everything!"

CHAPTER SEVEN

The woman in the uniform takes Lincoln's phone. "We can track the phone. We can find out where Eric is now."

"Yes Wanda," says Oscar. "Please do that. And please ask someone to look at the security cameras in the baggage claim area. Maybe we will see the woman who took the bag with the flower."

Wanda hurries out.

"I think I know what happened," says Clarissa. "The young woman is a member of a drug gang. She took the bag with the flower because she thought it was Lincoln's bag. She thought the drugs were inside. But it was not Lincoln's bag. Now you have the drugs, but the gang know they have the wrong bag. So they will come back to the airport and try again."

Oscar looks at her. "Are you a policewoman?" he asks.

Clarissa laughs. "I am seventy-six years old. I am a retired nurse, but I read a lot of mystery books!"

"You are in a lot of trouble," says Oscar to Lincoln. "How did you get the drugs from Mexico to Texas?"

Lincoln explains about the fruit and vegetables. "I go to Mexico every week. I have travel papers. I have been going for about twenty years. Everyone knows me."

"I don't think Lincoln is a bad man," says Clarissa. "He is like a baby. I don't think he knew anything about the drugs. I think he wanted to do something nice for his friend."

"I agree," says Oscar. "But he did a very bad thing. He is in a lot of trouble. But if he helps us, maybe it will be OK. Maybe we can catch a drug gang. If we are lucky, then everyone will be very kind to Lincoln."

Oscar, Clarissa and Lincoln wait.

Wanda comes into the room. She is very excited. "The police know the woman who took the wrong bag. Her name is Marcia McLean. Her boyfriend is called Eric Williams. He had a Facebook page, but he took it down months ago. We don't know anything about him. He doesn't have a job, but he travels a lot. Maybe he is a member of a drug gang. We must catch him!"

"Yes," says Oscar. "I think we can catch him. But Lincoln must help us."

"Lincoln," he says. "You must take your bag and stand by the Information Desk. You must wait for Eric. He will come soon, I think."

"Oh yes! But what about Eric's piñata? He will be angry with me."

"Don't worry about the piñata. Just go out there and wait for Eric."

Clarissa looks at Oscar. "It will be dangerous."

"Maybe it will be dangerous. But if Lincoln helps us, he will not be in trouble. And I want to catch this Eric Williams who tricked him!"

CHAPTER EIGHT

Lincoln stands by the Information Desk with his bag. He is unhappy.

There are many security guards in the area. They are watching, but they are not standing close to Lincoln. They don't want Eric to see them.

Lincoln sees a man run into the building. The man comes to him.

"Oh, it's you! Lincoln! I am so sorry! It has been a crazy day, and you have waited for a long time! But it's OK now. We can go. My car is parked on a taxi stand so we must be quick. Is this your bag?"

The man picks up the bag and hurries to the exit door. Lincoln goes with him. There is a car parked very close to the exit.

There is a young woman in the driver's seat. *That's the pretty woman who talked to me. The woman who asked me for water!* thinks Lincoln.

The man throws the bag into the back of the car. He says, "Thanks. You are an idiot, but you helped me. Goodbye!"

Lincoln is not very smart. But suddenly he understands. *This is not Eric from high school. This is a bad man. He thinks I am an idiot.*

Lincoln is very, very angry.

The security guards are running towards the car. Eric sees them and pulls out a gun. Lincoln sees the gun. He doesn't care. He runs at Eric. Eric fires the gun, but Lincoln doesn't stop. He picks him up and throws him on the ground.

The security guards run up. They put handcuffs on Eric and the young woman. They take them away.

The people from airport security and the police drug squad take

Lincoln to a small empty room and talk to him for hours and hours.

When her friend's flight arrives from Rome, Clarissa meets her, and says, "Please go to the hotel without me. I will come later."

"What are you doing?" asks her friend.

"I am helping a man from Texas. And I am having a lot of fun! It has been a very exciting day! Real life is more interesting than books!"

CHAPTER NINE

Clarissa is in Oscar's office with Wanda.

Wanda is very happy. "I can't believe it!" she says to Clarissa. "We have caught a big drug dealer. Everyone around the world was looking for him. We were looking for him here in the USA. But no one knew his name was Eric Williams, and he was living in New York City!"

Clarissa is worried about Lincoln.

"Poor Lincoln. Do you think we could do something to make him happy?" she asks. "Oscar says he is not in trouble now. He didn't know anything about the drugs, and he helped to catch the drug dealer."

"What can we do?" asks Wanda.

"Can you find the real Eric Williams? The one that went to school with Lincoln?"

"I will try. He will be about thirty-eight years old. He went to El Placido High School in Texas. Maybe I can find him," says Wanda.

"Please try," says Clarissa.

It is late at night. Lincoln is alone in the small empty room at the airport. He is tired and unhappy. He has a hole in his jacket - a bullet hole. *My mother gave me this jacket for my birthday. Now it has a hole in it. She will be angry,* he thinks.

Suddenly the door opens. Wanda and Clarissa come into the room. They are smiling.

"Surprise!" they shout.

There is a man standing behind them.

"Lincoln! Lincoln Berger! From El Placido High School! We were in the brass band together," he shouts.

"Uh. Who are you?" asks Lincoln.

"I am Eric Williams. We were in the same class in high school and now you are in New York. I live in Newark, New Jersey. I am married. I have four children. I want you to come and stay with me. I want to talk to you about high school days. Please come."

Lincoln stands up. "Can I go?" he asks Wanda.

"Yes. Oscar says you can go. Here is your bag. Have a nice time with your friend."

Eric and Lincoln walk out of the room. Lincoln is smiling.

Clarissa and Wanda are smiling too. "You did a great job," Clarissa says.

Wanda says, "I told Eric everything. He understands. He got in his car and drove here. He is a very nice man. Lincoln will have a great vacation."

Wanda and Clarissa are tired. They sit down.

"It was a good day," says Wanda. "We caught a drug dealer, and we helped Lincoln."

"Yes," says Clarissa. "I am old, and sometimes life is not interesting. But today was fun!"

THANK YOU

Thank you for reading Lincoln Takes a Trip. (Word count: 5,034) We hope you enjoyed it.

If you would like to read more graded readers, please visit our website http://www.italkyoutalk.com

Other Level 3 graded readers include
A Dangerous Weekend
A Holiday to Remember
Akiko and Amy Part 1
Akiko and Amy Part 2
Akiko and Amy Part 3
Be My Valentine
Different Seas
Enjoy Your Business Trip
Enjoy Your Homestay
I Need a Friend
Match Day
Old Jack's Ghost Stories from England (1)
Old Jack's Ghost Stories from England (2)
Old Jack's Ghost Stories from Ireland
Old Jack's Ghost Stories from Japan
Old Jack's Ghost Stories from Scotland
Old Jack's Ghost Stories from Wales
Party Time!

Pretty and Bright
Stories for Christmas
Summer Days
The Curse
The Diary
Time to Go
Together Again
Who is Holly?

ABOUT THE AUTHOR

I Talk You Talk Press is an award-winning Japan-based publisher of language textbooks, graded readers and language learning/teaching resources. We won the Language Learner Literature Award in 2019 and 2020.

Our team is made up of highly experienced language teachers and translators, who have all studied at least one additional language to an advanced level.

This experience enables us to design our materials from the perspective of both the teacher and the learner. We consult with both teachers and language learners when designing our textbooks and graded readers, and test our materials extensively in the classroom before publication.

We are a fast-growing press, and currently publish graded readers for learners of English. We publish new graded readers monthly.

www.ingramcontent.com/pod-product-compliance
Lightning Source LLC
LaVergne TN
LVHW042240190726
843491LV00003BA/1169

* 9 7 8 4 9 0 9 7 3 3 6 9 6 *